Fall Color Finder

A Pocket Guide to the More Colorful
Trees of Eastern North America

C. Ritchie Bell
Anne H. Lindsey

D0003504

Laurel Hill Press
Chapel Hill, N.C.

Acknowledgments

The authors have used certain design features and terminology from the book *Tree Finder*, with permission from the Nature Study Guild, Berkeley, California, and a number of photographs from their own *Fall Color and Woodland Harvests* with permission of Laurel Hill Press.

Text Photographic Credits
(see initials by pictures)

RRB   Richard R. Braham
BGH   Barbara G. Hallowell
HM   Hugh Morton
LO   Lowell Orbison
RVP   Rick Vande Poll
DHR   David H. Ramsey
RS   Robert Speas

Design by Kachergis Book Design, Pittsboro, NC

Printed by Bassett Printing, Bassett, VA

WILD CHERRY

SLIPPERY ELM

BLACKGUM

Why Leaves Have Different Shapes and Colors

Variation is a characteristic of all living organisms. The basic differences, or variations, among different kinds or species of plants and animals are hereditary, but individual organisms, trees for example, may show a lot of variation caused by their particular environment. Leaf size and leaf color are often easily modified (even on a single tree!) by such environmental factors as rainfall, temperature, and light intensity. However, such things as leaf arrangement (opposite or alternate), the general form of the leaf (lobed or unlobed), the leaf margins (smooth or toothed), the shape of the leaf tip (blunt or sharply pointed), and the relative length of the leaf stalk or petiole (long, short, or none) are all more constant characters within a particular species or kind of tree and are therefore good "key" characters to help you identify trees at any season. For example, compare the features and variation in the leaf silhouettes of Wild Cherry, Slippery Elm, and Blackgum to the left and also see Blackgum leaf color variation on page 27.

[3]

How To Use This Key

- Select a leaf of typical size, shape, and color from the tree you wish to identify. Avoid leaves that do not look "normal" or "average." A quick comparison of your leaf with the four sets of drawings on page 5 will give you most of the information - and terms - you will need to identify any of the more colorful fall trees quickly and correctly.

- Start at the top of page 6 with the first pair of identifying features, numbered **1.**

- Proceed step by step from one numbered pair to the next by taking the most appropriate of the two choices until you have a tree name and the photograph matches your leaf. If you come to an obvious "dead end" in the key or you are not comfortable with the identification, you can always go back to **1** and rework the leaf through the key.

- When you have made your final choice compare your leaf with the color photograph, the leaf outline, and the distribution map for that species to verify your identification. Keep in mind that many of the less common, or less colorful, trees could not be included in this small guide.

- Note: If you have only a single colorful leaf, you might be able to identify it more quickly by matching it with the colored silhouettes in the handy Shape/Color Index on pages 62-63.

Leaf Characters

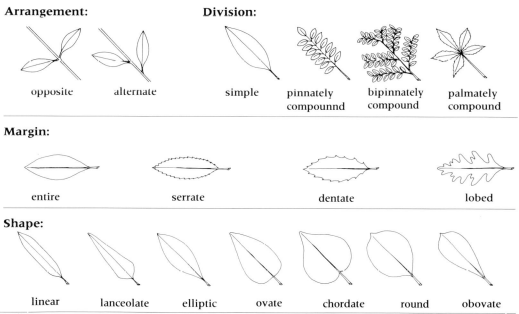

Arrangement:

opposite   alternate

Division:

simple   pinnately compounnd   bipinnately compound   palmately compound

Margin:

entire   serrate   dentate   lobed

Shape:

linear   lanceolate   elliptic   ovate   chordate   round   obovate

TAMARACK, *Larix laricina*

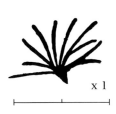

x 1

1 If the leaves are about 1 inch long, needle-like, and in clusters on short shoots, it is TAMARACK

If the leaves are flat, broad, and not needle-like, go to **2.**

2 If the leaves or buds are opposite on the twigs, go to **3.**

If the leaves or buds are alternate on the twigs, go to **11.**

3 | If the leaves are compound, composed of several leaflets, go to **4**.

If the leaves are simple, not composed of leaflets, go to **7**.

4 | If there are only 3 leaflets, or, if more, the leaflets are in two rows along the leaf stalk, go to **5**.

If there are 5 or more leaflets and they all radiate from the end of the leaf stalk, it is YELLOW BUCKEYE

The leaves of the OHIO BUCKEYE *(Aesculus glabra)* and our other three species of native Buckeyes are all quite similar.

YELLOW BUCKEYE, *Aesculus octandra*

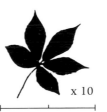

x 10

[7]

BOX ELDER, *Acer negundo*

x 8

[8]

5 If the 3-7 leaflets are coarsely toothed and of different sizes and shapes, it is
BOX ELDER

If the 7-9 leaflets are finely toothed and are similar in size and shape,　　go to **6.**

6 If the twigs and leaf stalks are hairy, it is
WHITE ASH

If the twigs and leaf stalks are not hairy, it is　　GREEN ASH

Related less colorful species, not illustrated are: BLACK ASH (*Fraxinus nigra*) with sessile (stalkless) leaflets and BLUE ASH (*Fraxinus quadrangulata*) with squarish stems.

WHITE ASH, *Fraxinus americana*

GREEN ASH, *Fraxinus pennsylvanica*

x 10

x 10

[9]

7

If the leaf is without teeth or lobes and has a single main vein with smaller side veins, it is   DOGWOOD

If the leaf is lobed and has 3 to 7 main veins radiating from one point at the base of the leaf, it is a Maple,   go to **8.**

DOGWOOD, *Cornus florida*

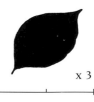

x 3

8

If the leaves appear to be 3-lobed rather than 5-lobed (the 2 basal lobes being small or absent), go to **9.**

If the leaves are distinctly 5-lobed (may be either yellow or red), it is
SUGAR MAPLE

In SILVER MAPLE (*Acer saccharinum*), a related and less colorful species also with 5-lobed leaves, the base of the terminal lobe is narrowed.

SUGAR MAPLE, *Acer saccharum*

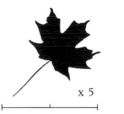

x 5

[11]

BLACK MAPLE, *Acer nigrum*

x 5

9

If the leaf stalk and under surface are hairy and the leaf margins seem to droop, it is BLACK MAPLE

If the leaf stalk and the under surface of the leaf are not hairy and the leaf margins are flat, go to **10.**

10

If the leaf margin is coarsely and irregularly toothed and the leaf base is not smoothly rounded in outline (leaves may be either red or yellow) and the young trunks are gray, it is RED MAPLE

If the leaf margin is finely doubly toothed and the leaf base is smoothly rounded in outline and the young trunks are green and white striped, it is
STRIPED or GOOSE-FOOT MAPLE

RED MAPLE, *Acer rubrum*

STRIPED MAPLE, *Acer pensylvanicum*

x 4

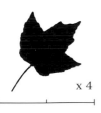

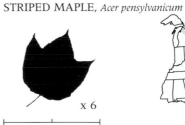

x 6

[13]

BLACK LOCUST, *Robinia pseudoacacia*

x 10

11 If the leaves are compound, composed of several leaflets, go to **12**.

If the leaves are simple, not composed of leaflets, go to **20**.

12 If the margins of the leaves are entire (that is, they are not toothed at all), go to **13**.

If the margins of the leaves are toothed, or partly toothed, go to **14**.

Note: with an early frost or with a dry autumn season the leaves of both Black Locust and Tree of Heaven (p. 16) may die and drop without turning color.

13 If the leaflets are about 2 inches long and rounded at each end, and there are paired thorns at the base of the leaf on young stems (fruits are flat dry bean pods), it is BLACK LOCUST

If the leaflets are over 2 inches long and definitely pointed (especially at the tip), and there are no thorns on young stems (fruits are clusters of white berries), go wash your hands; it is POISON SUMAC

POISON SUMAC, *Rhus vernix*

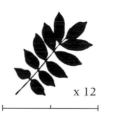

x 12

14

If the leaflets have only 2-3 irregular, basal, glandular teeth on each side and a disagreeable odor when crushed, it is
TREE OF HEAVEN

If the leaflets have numerous marginal teeth on both sides and are odorless (or the odor is pungent but not disagreeable) when crushed, go to **15**.

TREE OF HEAVEN, *Ailanthus altissima*

x 18

[16]

15 If the twigs are stout and covered with brown hairs and the small tree bears pointed terminal clusters of small hairy red fruits, it is   STAGHORN SUMAC

If the twigs and fruit are not as above,
go to **16.**

STAGHORN SUMAC, *Rhus typhina*   [RS]

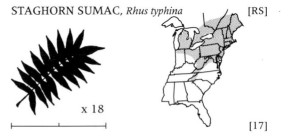

x 18

[17]

BLACK WALNUT, *Juglans nigra*

x 18

[18]

16 If the leaf is 1-2 feet long with more than 12 leaflets and the twigs have brown pith in flat plates (not solid), it is
BLACK WALNUT

If the leaf is less than 12" long (or longer but with fewer leaflets and the terminal leaflet distinctly larger than the others) and the twigs have solid pith, go to **17.**

17 If the leaf has 13-17 leaflets that are smooth beneath and the small tree has flat clusters of orange or red fruits, it is
MOUNTAIN ASH

If the leaf has 11 or fewer leaflets that are either smooth or hairy beneath and the large tree bears brown, hard-shelled nuts, it is a Hickory, go to **18.**

MOUNTAIN ASH, *Sorbus americana*

[RS]

[BGH]

x 12

[19]

MOCKERNUT HICKORY, *Carya tomentosa*

x 10

18 If there are 7-9 leaflets, densely hairy beneath, and the end leaflet is obviously larger and the nuts have thick husks, it is MOCKERNUT HICKORY

If there are 5 (rarely 7) leaflets that are smooth beneath and all about the same size, and the nuts have thin husks,
go to **19.**

19 If the bark of the tree is loose in long shaggy strips, it is SHAGBARK HICKORY

If the bark is tight, furrowed, not in loose shaggy strips, it is PIGNUT HICKORY

A similar and equally colorful species, with 7-11 leaflets, is BITTERNUT HICKORY (*Carya cordiformis*).

SHAGBARK HICKORY, *Carya ovata*

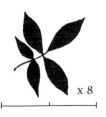

x 8

PIGNUT HICKORY, *Carya glabra*

x 8

20 If the leaf is smoothly heart-shaped with veins branching from the base, it is
REDBUD

If the leaf is not as above, go to **21.**

21 If the leaf is long and slender, about 5 times as long as wide, go to **22.**

If the leaf is not long and slender,
go to **23.**

REDBUD, *Cercis canadensis*

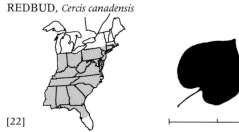

x 3

[22]

22 If the leaf tapers evenly to a long pointed tip, and has small marginal teeth, it is
BLACK WILLOW

If the leaf is more abruptly tapered to a blunt point with a single bristle at the tip and has smooth margins, it is
WILLOW OAK

BLACK WILLOW, *Salix nigra*

x 4

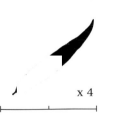

WILLOW OAK, *Quercus phellos*

x 3

[23]

CUCUMBER TREE, *Magnolia acuminata*

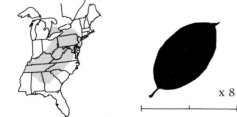

[24]

x 8

23

If the margin of the leaf has teeth or if the leaf is deeply or shallowly lobed,
go to **27**.

If the leaf has neither teeth nor lobes,
go to **24**.

24

If the leaf is 5" to 20" long and neither thick nor shiny, go to **25**.

If the leaf is 2" to 5" long, somewhat thick and shiny, go to **26**.

25

If the leaf is ovate or elliptic and if there is a line or scar completely encircling the twig at each leaf, it is

CUCUMBER TREE

If the leaf is widest beyond the middle (obovate) and there is no line or scar around the twig at each leaf, it is

PAWPAW

PAWPAW, *Asimina triloba*

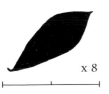

x 8

PERSIMMON, *Diospyros virginiana*

x 4

26 If the leaves are widest at the middle with conspicuous veins and the tree bears fleshy orange fruits about 1" in diameter, it is PERSIMMON

If the leaves are widest beyond the middle and the fruits of the tree are small and black or very dark blue, it is BLACKGUM OR TUPELO

27 If the leaf is deeply or shallowly lobed, or is lobed and also has teeth on the margin, go to **28.**

If the leaf is unlobed and the margin is finely or coarsely toothed, or doubly toothed, go to **41.**

BLACK GUM, *Nyssa sylvatica*

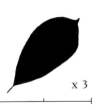

x 3

[27]

FRASER MAGNOLIA, *Magnolia fraseri*

x 8

28 If the leaf has both lobes and marginal teeth,　　　　　　　　go to **29**.

If the leaf has smooth lobes and no marginal teeth,　　　　　　go to **30**.

29 If the lateral lobes are more or less paired along the sides of the leaf and the leaf is longer than wide (and generally widest at or above the middle),　　go to **36**.

If the lobes all radiate from the base of the leaf and the leaf is about as long as wide (and generally widest below the middle),　　　　　　　go to **40**.

30 If the leaf is large, 8" to 12" or more long, is widest toward the tip, and has only two lobes (or "ears") near the base, it is FRASER MAGNOLIA

If the leaf is smaller and has 2 or more lobes (a wavy margin is considered to be shallowly lobed) that are not just basal "ears," or if some of the leaves on the tree are unlobed, go to **31**.

31 If the leaf is as wide as long and has 4 (rarely 6) prominent lobes and the broad apex is notched, it is TULIP POPLAR

If the leaf is not as above, go to **32**.

TULIP POPLAR, *Liriodendron tulipifera*

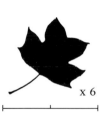

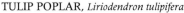 x 6

SASSAFRAS, *Sassafras albidum*   [RS]

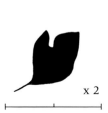

x 2

[30]

32 If some of the leaves on the tree are unlobed and others have either 2 or 3 lobes and if the twigs are green and aromatic, it is   SASSAFRAS

If the leaves of one tree are more uniform and have the same general number and pattern of lobes,   go to **33.**

33 If the numerous, shallow, rounded lobes form a wavy margin and the round leaf has an uneven (oblique) base, the small tree is   WITCH HAZEL

If the lobes are numerous and shallow and the leaf is longer than wide and tapers evenly to the base or if there are 5-9 rounded lobes with indentations 1/4 to 3/4 the distance from the margin to the midrib, it is an Oak,   go to **34.**

WITCH HAZEL, *Hamamelis virginiana*

x 4

CHESTNUT OAK, *Quercus prinus*

x 6

34

If the lobes are numerous, even, and shallow, it is

CHESTNUT OAK

If there are 5-9 unequal rounded lobes with deep sinuses, go to **35.**

35

If the 3 end lobes are by far the largest and somewhat square, giving the leaf the shape of a cross, it is POST OAK

If the lobes are more nearly the same size and proportion, though often somewhat variable from leaf to leaf, it is

WHITE OAK

POST OAK, *Quercus stellata*

WHITE OAK, *Quercus alba*

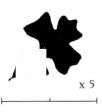

x 5

x 7

SPANISH OAK, *Quercus falcata*

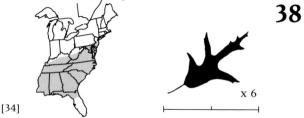

x 6

36 If the end lobe is long (about 1/3 to 1/2 the length of the blade) and slender, it is SPANISH OAK

If the end lobe is not long and slender, go to **37**.

37 If the leaf is deeply lobed (the sinuses cut over 1/2 the distance from the margin to the midrib), go to **38**.

If the leaf is shallowly lobed, go to **39**.

38 If the lobes taper toward their tips and the space between lobes is V-shaped, it is PIN OAK

If the lobes broaden toward their tips, forming oval spaces between lobes, and the midrib is yellow, it is SCARLET OAK

PIN OAK, *Quercus palustris*

x 4

SCARLET OAK, *Quercus coccinea*

x 6

[35]

BLACK OAK, *Quercus velutina*

x 7

39

If the leaf is thick, leathery, usually widening toward the tip, often 7-lobed, somewhat hairy beneath (the tree may have several different forms of leaves), and the buds are angled, it is

BLACK OAK

If the leaf is thin, firm, smooth beneath, 5" to 9" long, with lobes that taper toward their tips, usually more than 7-lobed, it is RED OAK

The leaves of BEAR OAK or SCRUB OAK (*Quercus ilicifolia*) are white-downy beneath and the tree is small, often in clumps or thickets.

RED OAK, *Quercus rubra* [BGH]

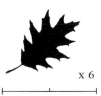

x 6

[37]

40 If the 3 to 5 lobes are indistinct, the marginal teeth variable and coarse, and the upper trunk of the tree is chalk white, it is   SYCAMORE

If the 5 lobes are quite distinct (the leaves star-like) with fine, even marginal teeth and the upper trunk of the tree is not white, it is   SWEETGUM

SYCAMORE, *Platanus occidentalis*

x 6

[38]

SWEETGUM, *Liquidambar styraciflua*

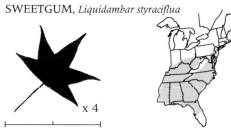

x 4

[39]

AMERICAN CHESTNUT, *Castanea dentata*

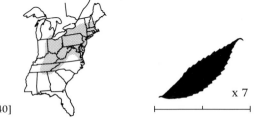

x 7

41

If the leaf is 5" to 7" or more long and narrowly elliptic (widest at middle and tapered evenly to base and apex, and 3 times, or more, as long as broad),

go to **42**.

If the leaf is less then 5" long or is not narrowly elliptic, go to **43**.

Note: When Chinese Chestnuts, which are immune to the Chestnut blight, were brought into this country about 1900, the blight came with them and slowly spread through the American forests. The magnificent American Chestnut trees that provided the early colonists with food, fuel, shelter, fences, and tannin for their leather clothes disappeared. Today only small "stump sprouts" are found.

42 If the leaf has prominent teeth at the ends of the strongly parallel lateral veins and the leaf is yellow to bronze or brown, it is   AMERICAN CHESTNUT

If the leaf has very small teeth and the lateral veins are not prominent and strongly parallel and the leaf is dark red, it is   SOURWOOD

SOURWOOD, *Oxydendrum arboreum*

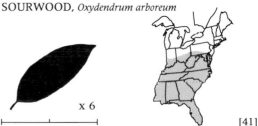

x 6

43

If the leaf is narrowly elliptic and 2" to 5" long with 2 or 3 small red glands at the base of the leaf or on the end of the leaf stalk and the leaves have the strong smell of almonds when crushed, it is
WILD CHERRY or BLACK CHERRY

If the leaf is not as above, go to **44.**

The closely related FIRE CHERRY or PIN CHERRY (*Prunus pensylvanica*) has a cluster of terminal buds and the leaves are hairless beneath along the mid-vein.

WILD CHERRY, *Prunus serotina*

x 3

44 | If the leaf stalk is long, about 1/2 or more as long as the blade, go to **45**.

If the leaf stalk is short, about 1/4 or less the length of the blade, go to **47**.

45 | If the leaf is rather widely elliptic and with scattered hairs (need hand lens!) on the petiole or leaf stalk, it is SERVICEBERRY

If the leaf is ovate and without hairs on the petiole, go to **46**.

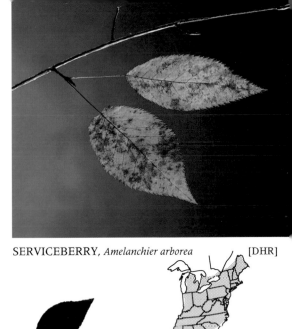

SERVICEBERRY, *Amelanchier arborea* [DHR]

x 4

[43]

46

If the leaf is about as long as wide and the teeth are small and numerous, it is TREMBLING ASPEN

If the leaf is somewhat longer than wide and the teeth are coarse and fewer in number, it is BIG-TOOTHED ASPEN

The equally colorful golden-yellow leaves of COTTONWOOD (*Populus deltoides*) are triangular with a straight base.

TREMBLING ASPEN, *Populus tremuloides*

x 2

47

If the side veins are prominent, numerous, straight, evenly spaced, and parallel,
go to **51**.

If the side veins are not as above,
go to **48**.

BIG-TOOTHED ASPEN, *Populus grandidentata* [LO]

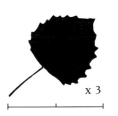

x 3

48 If the base of the leaf is uneven (oblique), go to **49.**

If the base of the leaf is even, go to **50.**

HACKBERRY, *Celtis occidentalis*

x 2

49 If the leaf is lance-shaped, widest at the base and with essentially straight edges tapering uniformly to a sharply pointed tip, it is HACKBERRY

If the leaf is widely ovate, or heart-shaped, widest about the middle with curving edges to a blunt tip, it is BASSWOOD

Note: with an early frost or with a dry autumn season the leaves of both Hackberry and Basswood may die and drop without turning color.

BASSWOOD, *Tilia heterophylla*

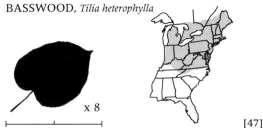

x 8

[47]

50

If the leaf is smooth and the marginal teeth obvious (some leaves may also be lobed), it is the introduced
WHITE MULBERRY

If the leaf is rough or scurfy and the marginal teeth are small and indistinct (some leaves may also be lobed), it is
RED MULBERRY

The leaves of the PAPER MULBERRY (*Broussonetia papyrifera*), introduced from China, where the leaves are used to feed silkworms, are very similar, but the twigs of this small tree are rough-hairy.

WHITE MULBERRY, *Morus alba*

x 5

RED MULBERRY, *Morus rubra*

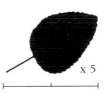

x 5

[49]

IRONWOOD, *Carpinus caroliniana*

x 3

51

If the bark of the tree is smooth, tight, and gray, go to **52.**

If the bark of the tree is not as above, go to **53.**

52

If the trunk of the small tree has muscle-like ridges under the bark and the small marginal teeth are more numerous than the side veins, it is

MUSCLEWOOD or IRONWOOD

If the trunk of the tree is smooth, without ridges under the bark, and the number of marginal teeth equals the number of side veins, it is AMERICAN BEECH

AMERICAN BEECH, *Fagus grandifolia*

[BGH]

x 3

[51]

HOP HORNBEAM, *Ostrya virginiana* [RVP]

x 3

53 If the bark of the tree is generally smooth, peeling, and white, gray, silver, pink, tan, or brown, or the twigs are aromatic, the tree is a Birch, go to **57.**

If the bark of the tree is rough, tight (not peeling), and tan or brown, go to **54.**

54 If the base of the leaf is even and the marginal teeth are small and very numerous, it is HOP HORNBEAM

If the base of the leaf is uneven (oblique) and the leaf is scurfy above (or if the bark of some of the young branches has corky ridges or "wings"), it is an Elm, go to **55.**

55 If the base of the leaf is only slightly uneven and if some of the young branches
have corky "wings," it is

WINGED ELM

If the base of the leaf is strongly uneven
(oblique) and the leaf is scurfy above,

go to **56.**

WINGED ELM, *Ulmus alata*

x 2

[53]

56 If the leaf is rough beneath as well as above and if the tip narrows abruptly, it is RED ELM or SLIPPERY ELM

If the leaf is smooth beneath (and either smooth or rough above) and narrowed gradually to the tip, it is

AMERICAN ELM

SLIPPERY ELM, *Ulmus rubra*

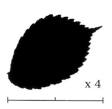

x 4

AMERICAN ELM, *Ulmus americana*

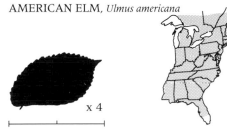

x 4

57

If the bark is dark brown and tight or is silvery-gray to yellow-gray and peeling in thin, curly strips, and the twigs are aromatic, go to **58.**

If the peeling bark is chalk-white or if some layers of the inner bark are light tan or rose-brown and the twigs are not aromatic, go to **59.**

CHERRY BIRCH, *Betula lenta*

x 3

58 If the bark is dark brown and not peeling, it is
  CHERRY BIRCH or SWEET BIRCH

If the bark is silver-gray to yellow-gray and peeling in thin, curly strips, it is
  YELLOW BIRCH

YELLOW BIRCH, *Betula alleghaniensis* [HM]

x 3

[57]

59

If the light gray bark of the young trunk peels and shows an inner layer of tan or rose-brown bark and if the tree grows in lowlands near creeks, ponds, or rivers, it is RIVER BIRCH

If the bark of the trunk is chalk-white and if the tree grows on upland slopes, it is PAPER BIRCH or CANOE BIRCH

The leaves of the colorful and closely related GRAY BIRCH (*Betula populifolia*) of New England are triangular in shape.

RIVER BIRCH, *Betula nigra*

x 2

[RS]

PAPER BIRCH, *Betula papyrifera*

[BGH]

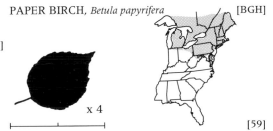

x 4

[59]

Index

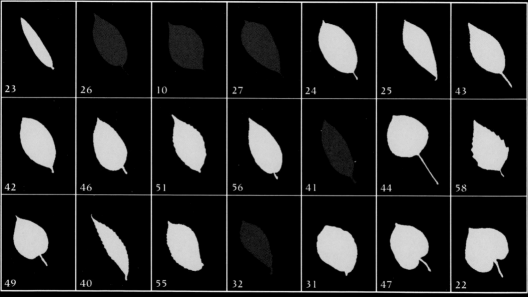

23 26 10 27 24 25 43
42 46 51 56 41 44 58
49 40 55 32 31 47 22

62]

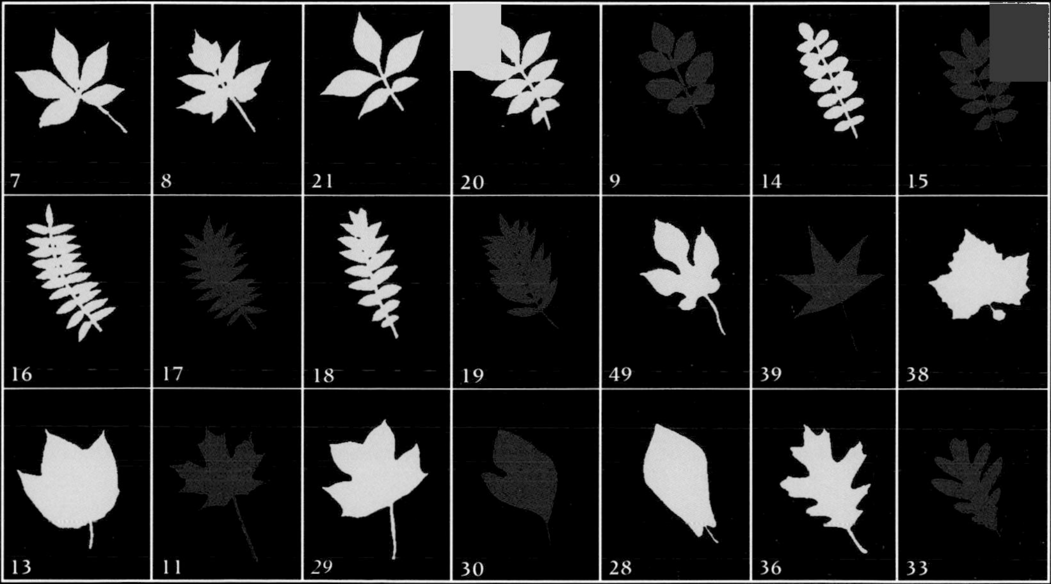
7
8
21
20
9
14
15
16
17
18
19
49
39
38
13
11
29
30
28
36
33

Field Notes